Hearing God's Voice For Kids

Hearing God's Voice For Kids Journal

Hearing God's Voice For Kids

Kathy Campbell

KINGDOM PUBLISHERS

4647 Reservoir Rd.
Geneseo, New York 14454

Preface

Now more than ever before we need to press into hearing what the Spirit of the Lord is saying today. We need to know Him. This manual will help your child/children in their journey of intimacy with the Lord and bring them to greater understanding of the commands in Scripture to encourage one another through the gift of prophecy.

I often will say as I instruct ones in the prophetic that all of the gifts of the Spirit flow through the prophetic. Being a prophetic person is one who is able to hear from God. We all hear from God to a certain extent.

The sons of Issachar had understanding of the times and they knew what to do. Having understanding of the times is equal to having words of wisdom, words of knowledge, and discernment flowing through you. When we hear God speaking then we are able to hear words of wisdom by the Spirit. When we hear God speaking then we are able to hear words of knowledge. When we hear God speaking then we are able to have discernment. When we hear God speaking then we are able to have faith to declare those things that are not as though they are. When we hear God speaking then we are able to have all of the Gifts of the Spirit flow through us.

Hearing God's Voice For Kids Journal

INTRODUCTION AND INSTRUCTION TO PARENTS AND/OR FACILITATORS

This manual has been written in such a way that the manual and its activations can be completed with your own child/children or with a group of children. The beginning group of Scriptures will be reviewed throughout the manual to help reinforce the basis for hearing from God. Many times we use repetition in this manual. Repetition helps us to remember what we are learning.

It is important to stress that "everyone" can hear God speak. There is not a big Holy Spirit or a little Holy Spirit but there is one Holy Spirit.

Children have a unique ability to hear from the Lord. There was a time when I was in Kansas City at a conference and had a prophetic word given to me that I would teach God's people how to have fun, fun, fun, in His house. A couple of years later, a mom in our church asked her two year old daughter to pray and ask the Lord to speak a word to her for me. The two year old bowed her head and closed her eyes while the mom prayed. The mom then asked the two year old what the Lord spoke to her for me and she said- fun, fun, fun. At that moment I realized the importance of teaching children to hear the voice of the Lord. Those three words from that two year old were so encouraging to me at that time. She knew nothing of the word I had received in Kansas City a couple of years prior.

Once after teaching this class to a group of children I had the parents come in the class to let the children hear from the Lord for them. In one activation I had the children face the front wall and close their eyes. Behind each of them I placed a parent and had the parent place their hand on the shoulder of the child they were standing behind. Behind one young girl I had placed a pastor. This young girl said she felt that this "person" wants to dance in worship and she said God loves it that he wants to dance in worship. To make a long story short, this pastor had just prayed that morning and talked to the Lord about his desire to dance in worship before Him.

It is also important that once you train your child/children to hear God speak that you provide an opportunity for them to develop that gift to hear from God. We provide a once a month meeting where the children who take the class can exercise their gift to hear from God for others. We like it best to have an adult and a child team. We all need an outlet and children are no exception.

There are many opportunities we can use to help train our children to minister the heart of God to others. Perhaps while sitting at a restaurant with your child you can encourage your child to ask the Lord to speak to them for the waiter or waitress. Other places we have taken children to minister are Nursing Homes, Hospitals, Parks, etc. There was a time when I felt the Lord wanted me to visit someone in their home (whom I did not know) and pray for them. I took along a child with me on this visit. We knocked on the door and waited for someone to answer the door. The child I had with me was totally fine and not nervous while I on the other hand was shaking. The folks opened the door and we were invited in. I told the people that I felt the Lord wanted me to come and pray with them if they were open. They were so happy to have us come and pray. The wife had just had a stroke and was afraid of having another one. The child and I both prayed. What blessed this couple the most was that a child laid his hand on them and prayed and they felt the love of God. Tears and hugs were shared.

From time to time visitors have been disappointed to see that a child will be ministering to them. But after the ministry there has never been a person leave disappointed. But every person comes back and says that they hope the next time they come for ministry that a child is on the team. Children can say things that adults cannot. There is an innocence and purity that they possess. For example, a child was ministering to an adult concerning their best friend. The child went on to say that they loved their best friend, spent a lot of time with their best friend, and did not want to say good-by to their best friend but knew that they needed to let their best friend go. The child then went on to say that the person's best friend was sickness. The adult being ministered to shared that the word the child had given was right and that they had allowed sickness to be their best friend.

On page 32 is an activation for the children to hear the Father's heart for themselves individually. They will take the time to listen to what the Father is saying to them. This will be a very pleasant experience for many children. Some children may need help in beginning to think that God loves them so much. With very little coaxing you will see a child's countenance light up as they understand that God does love them. One child took the class and wrote these words- *"He said to me- you sing beautiful- I almost started to cry- I could not believe it- it was like a miracle had just happened to me."*

One other thing we do is provide "prizes" at the end of the class time to encourage the children to participate. The prizes though small are a great incentive to help the children volunteer in the activations. Over and over children have asked when we will come back to do the class again. It is a fun and important event for children to learn to how to hear the voice of God. A chart can be kept to keep track of the points.

- ✓ The instructions will be easy to follow. They will be in black and italicized. And there will be the red checkmark.

The version of the Bible used is the New King James Version.

The Answer Key is at the back of the manual on page 47.

Hearing God's Voice For Kids Journal

Scriptures to Know

✓ *Read out loud together*

1 Corinthians 14:1
Pursue love, and desire spiritual gifts, but especially that you may prophesy.

1 Corinthians 14:31
For you can all prophesy one by one, that all may learn and all may be encouraged.

Ephesians 5:1
Therefore be imitators of God as dear children.

1 Peter 4:10
As each one has received a gift, minister it to one another, as good stewards of the manifold grace of God.

Hearing God's Voice For Kids Journal

✓ Read the verse and then ask for volunteers to fill in each blank space.
A white board can be used to help the children spell the answers correctly.

1 Corinthians 14:1

P_____ LOVE

And

D_____

Spiritual gifts

But

Especially

That you may

P_____

Hearing God's Voice For Kids Journal

✓ *Read the verse and then ask for volunteers to fill in each blank space.
A white board can be used to help the children spell the answers correctly.*

Ephesians 5:1

Therefore be

I_____

Of

God

As

Dear

C_____

Hearing God's Voice For Kids Journal

✓ Read the verse and then ask for volunteers to fill in each blank space.
A white board can be used to help the children spell the answers correctly.

1 Peter 4:10

As each o_____

has received a g_____,

M_____ it (helping)

to one another

As good s_____

of the manifold grace of God.

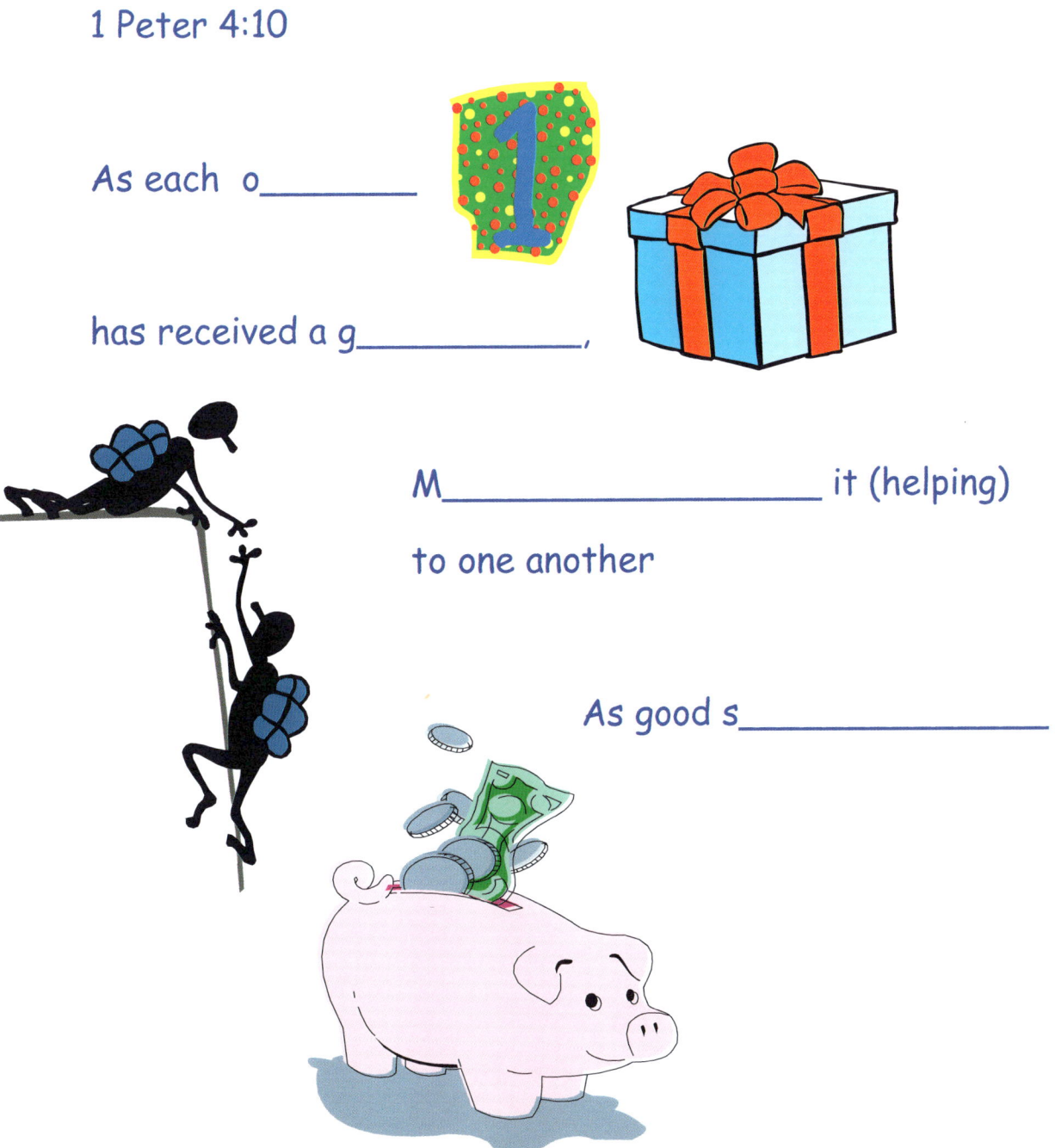

9

Hearing God's Voice For Kids Journal

There are nine gifts of the Holy Spirit listed in 1 Corinthians 12:8-10.

✓ *Read the verses and then ask for volunteers to fill in each blank space. A white board can be used to help the children spell the answers correctly.*

#1- W_____ of Wisdom

#2- W_____ of Knowledge

#3- F_____

#4- G_____s of Healings

#5- W_____ of Miracles

#6- P_____

#7- D_____ of spirits

#8- D_____ kinds of tongues

#9- I_____ of tongues

How to be used in the Gifts of the Holy Spirit:

✓ *Read Ezekiel 40:4 and Ezekiel 44:5*
  Say aloud the following-

LOOK TO SEE

LISTEN TO HEAR

  **SENSE TO FEEL**

✓ *Children can be trained to see a picture in their minds eye or to listen to what the Lord might be saying or even to have a sense of what some might feel at any given time. One way to begin to train is to ask the children to close their eyes and pray that the Lord give them a picture with their eyes closed. After a minute or two have the children open their eyes and ask who saw a picture. As children begin to share it will encourage others that what they saw was significant and that God wants to speak through them.*

Hearing God's Voice For Kids Journal

✓ *In this activation the children can either lie on the floor or lay their heads on a table while a worship song is being played. It works best to have them close their eyes. After the song is finished ask the children to write down anything they felt while the song was playing. Then discuss what they wrote down in the manual.*

First- Everyone find a quiet spot to lie down and listen as a worship song is played.

Then- List some ways we might feel when the Holy Spirit comes.

For example:

I feel funny inside. Or- I feel happy. Or- I feel tears come to my eyes.

How else might we feel?

_____
_____
_____
_____
_____
_____
_____
_____

✓ *It is important to review the steps to take in beginning to hear God speak to us.*

Steps to take:

#1- Tell the Holy Spirit you love Him
=WORSHIP & RELATIONSHIP

#2- Ask the Holy Spirit to come
=Make ROOM for Him

#3- Wait quietly
=Looking, Listening, Feeling

Why do we do this?

We want to be like

This is activation on the value of working together on a team. Children need to know that they are on the Lord's team. The Lord desires for us to hear from Him so that others can be encouraged. We can actually work with the Lord to encourage others. The obvious message in this activation is that we need each other. After going through the activation and talking about working with the Lord on His team and needing each other you might want to have some fun competition.

- ✓ *Children pair off and sit back to back, lock arms and stand up together.*

Hearing God's Voice For Kids Journal

- ✓ Read again verses 8-10 of 1 Corinthians 12.
  It is fun and important to add motions to the gifts listed as reinforcement to help remember what the gifts are. Children will need to stand while doing the motions. Review the motions a few times doing them slow at first and then speed it up.

Motions for the nine gifts of the Holy Spirit-

Word of Wisdom- with index finger pointed at the temple say, Word of Wisdom.

Word of Knowledge- with hand at the side of mouth and motioning forward say, Word of Knowledge.

Faith- right fist smacks into open left hand and say, Faith.

Gifts of Healings- while arms and hands are outstretched (as in laying hands on the sick) say, Gifts of Healings.

Working of Miracles- with arms reaching up and waving, say, Working of Miracles. (When a miracle happens we typically raise our hands and shout hallelujah!)

Prophecy- with arms at side and palms facing forward, we will lift them (as though we are carrying something in our arms) and say, Prophecy. Prophecy can be like helping someone along.

Discerning of spirits- with arms at our side, we move our right hand out in an outward flip motion and then our left hand to the other side in an outward flip motion and say, Discerning of Spirits.

Different Kinds of Tongues- extend the left hand straight out, palm up, in front of you and say Different Kinds of Tongues.

Interpretation of Tongues- extend the right hand straight out, palm down, in front of you and close over the left hand (clasping hands together) and say, Interpretation of Tongues.
Explain that the last two gifts listed go together thus the hands come together.

✓ *More review of the Gifts of the Holy Spirit listed in 1 Corinthians 12:8-10. Ask for volunteers to fill in the answers in the blank spaces.*

The nine gifts of the Holy Spirit are:

#1- W_____ of Wisdom

#2- W_____ of Knowledge

#3- F_____

#4- G_____s of Healings

#5- W_____ of Miracles

#6- P_____

#7- D_____ of spirits

#8- D_____ kinds of tongues

#9- I_____ of tongues

Hearing God's Voice For Kids Journal

✓ It is important to review ways that God might speak to us. It might be through a picture we see in the room or a picture in our minds eye. We might hear a word or think of a word. Or we might feel something inside. There are many ways that God can speak to us. As we focus on these three avenues, eyes, ears, and senses, it will help us to develop or fine tune our ability to hear God.

What is it we do?

Look to ____ ____ ____

Listen to ____ ____ ____ ____

Sense to ____ ____ ____ ____

Hearing God's Voice For Kids Journal

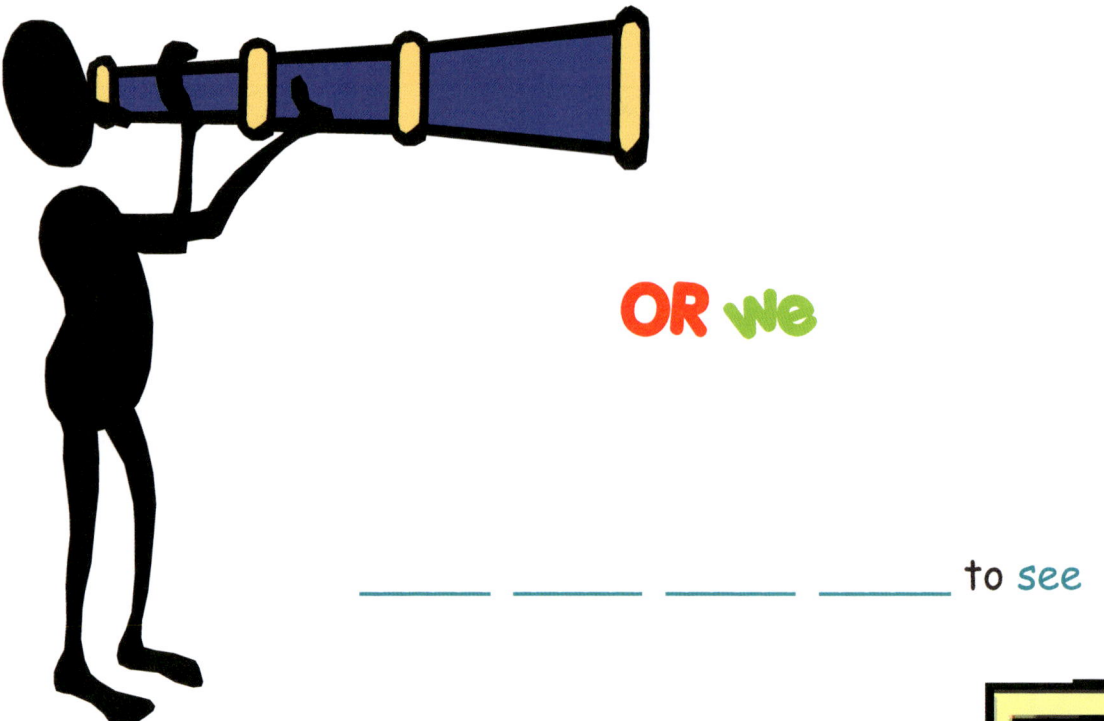

OR we

____ ____ ____ ____ to see

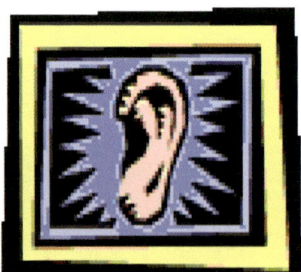

____ ____ ____ ____ ____ to hear

____ ____ ____ ____ ____ to feel

Hearing God's Voice For Kids Journal

✓ In this activation we will seek to encourage our neighbor. We will need to exchange manuals with someone. Be sure that names are on the manual so they get returned to the right individual.

Let's tell the Holy Spirit we love Him.

This is the same as **Worship**

Let's ask the Holy Spirit to come.

And then...

✓ *Before beginning to play a worship song make sure manuals have been exchanged. Once manuals have been exchanged, pray and tell the Holy Spirit we love Him and we want Him to come. Begin the worship song while praying. After the song has played the children will write encouraging words in their neighbor's manual. If done at home, you can have your child/children take turns encouraging each other or yourself.*

What do you feel?

Dear _____

_____

_____

_____

_____

_____

_____

_____

_____

_____

_____

Hearing God's Voice For Kids Journal

Who do we want to be like?

- ✓ Activation-Five volunteers needed at one time. Face each volunteer at the front of the room with their back to the class or other participants. Each volunteer keeps their eyes closed during this activation of encouragement. Behind each volunteer place an individual and they lightly place their hand on the volunteers shoulder without talking. Pray for the volunteer and ask God to speak encouragement to those standing behind. Then let the volunteers share one by one. After sharing they can turn around and see who they encouraged. Even adult helpers can be placed behind the volunteers.

  If done at home you can place a sibling or friend or neighbor behind your child with them not knowing who is behind them.

✓ *Review the basis for hearing the voice of the Lord through the Scriptures. Read aloud. Ask for volunteers to fill in the blank spaces.*

1 Corinthians 14:31

For _____ can _____ prophesy one by one, that _____ may learn and _____ may be encouraged.

Who can prophesy?

_____

What does prophecy do?

_____

✓ More review. Ask for volunteers to fill in the blank spaces.

1 Corinthians 14:1

Pursue _____,

And desire spiritual _____,

but especially that you may

_____.

- ✓ Activation- exchange manuals again. Once again, explain that the Lord desires for us to encourage each other. The way to begin or the way to take steps to hear from God is through worship and relationship with Him. We express our love to the Lord and ask Him to come and help us to be an encouragement to each other. While the worship song is playing have the children write words of encouragement. If done at home, you can have your child/children take turns encouraging each other or yourself.

What is God saying to you now?

Dear_____

_____

_____

_____

_____

_____

- ✓ Blanket Activation- this is completed best if done in a group. Either have all the children stand on a blanket or have it be a match between the boys and the girls by having the boys stand on one blanket and all the girls stand on another blanket. With no one stepping off the blanket, the children work together as a team and turn the blanket over. If anyone touches the floor by moving off the blanket they are out of the game.
This activation will emphasize the need for team participation.
- ✓ Questions to ask when activation is complete-
Was there a leader?
Who became the leader?
How important was it to follow instructions?
What happened when someone did not follow instructions?

The point of this activation is to emphasize the need for following instruction and being part of a team.

Hearing God's Voice For Kids Journal

✓ *God will speak to us many times using pictures. We can help children pay attention to the pictures they see by emphasizing that God speaks through pictures we see around us or pictures in our minds eye. The following pictures will help us to think about what God might say through what we see. These activations can be completed with our own child/children or in a group of children. If you have a larger group of children you might want to divide the children into smaller groups and encourage participation. This first picture can be used as an example before dividing into smaller groups. Have children take turns sharing their thoughts on the picture. This will help to prompt the children to think about each picture given.*

What do you think God could be saying in this picture?

_____

_____

_____

_____

_____

Hearing God's Voice For Kids Journal

✓ *Space is provided to write down any thoughts on the following pictures.*

What do you think God could be saying in each of these pictures?

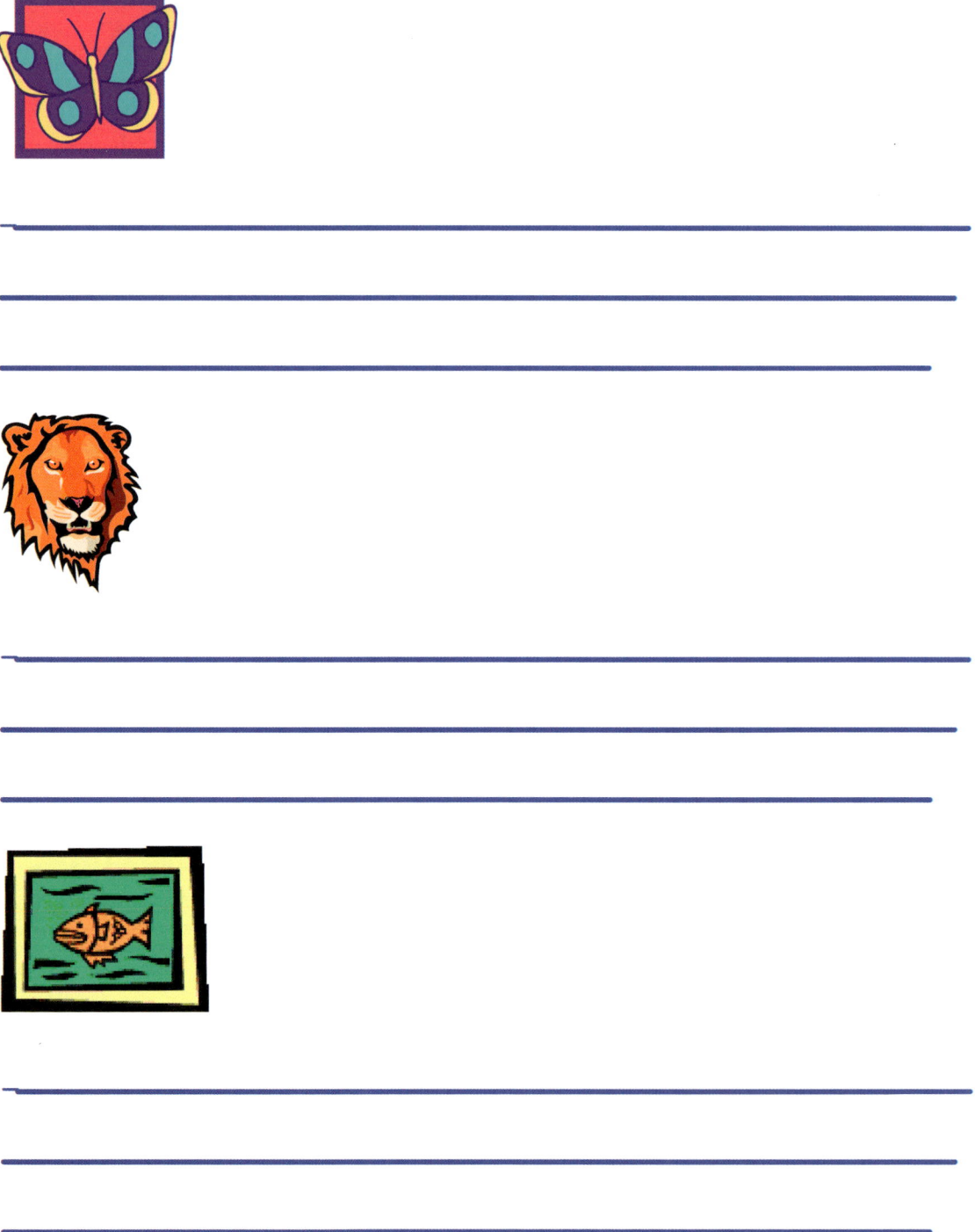

_____

_____

_____

_____

_____

_____

_____

_____

_____

Hearing God's Voice For Kids Journal

✓ In small groups discuss the following pictures. Instruct everyone to choose at least one picture and encourage someone in their group using that picture as a reference.

What do you think God could be saying in these pictures?

Hearing God's Voice For Kids Journal

✓ Ask for volunteers. Instruct volunteers to choose at least one picture and encourage someone in the class using that picture as a reference.

What do you think God could be saying to someone sitting by you in these pictures?

Hearing God's Voice For Kids Journal

✓ In this activation we will ask the Holy Spirit to speak to us through a picture. After seeing a picture in their minds eye, the children will then draw the picture. Remember to always follow the steps in beginning to hear the voice of God- worship is a key.

Draw the picture you see.

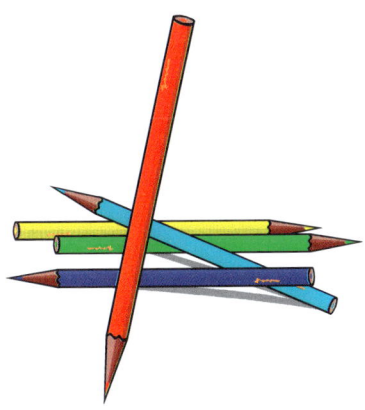

Hearing God's Voice For Kids Journal

- Have the children stand and recite the nine gifts using the motions and then fill in the blanks.

The nine gifts of the Holy Spirit are:

#1- Word of W_____

#2- Word of K_____

#3- F_____

#4- Gifts of H_____

#5- Working of M_____

#6- P_____

#7- Discerning of s_____

#8- Different kinds of t_____

#9- Interpretation of t_____

Hearing God's Voice For Kids Journal

- ✓ In this activation characters needed are a **narrator**, Philip, Nathanael, and Jesus. Each character reads their part.

Our goal is to be like Jesus.
Jesus flowed in the gifts of the Spirit.
Here is one example from Scripture:

John 1:45-51

Narrator- Philip found Nathanael and said to him,

Philip- "We have found Him of whom Moses in the law, and also the prophets, wrote--Jesus of Nazareth, the son of Joseph."

Narrator- And Nathanael said to him,

Nathanael- "Can anything good come out of Nazareth?"

Narrator- Philip said to him,

Philip- "Come and see."

Narrator- Jesus saw Nathanael coming toward Him, and said of him,

Jesus- "Behold, an Israelite indeed, in whom is no deceit!"

Narrator- Nathanael said to Him,

Nathanael- "How do You know me?"

Narrator- Jesus answered and said to him,

Jesus- "Before Philip called you, when you were under the fig tree, I saw you."

Narrator- Nathanael answered and said to Him,

Nathanael- "Rabbi, You are the Son of God! You are the King of Israel!"

Narrator- Jesus answered and said to him,

Jesus- "Because I said to you, 'I saw you under the fig tree,' do you believe? You will see greater things than these." And He said to him, "Most assuredly, I say to you, hereafter you shall see heaven open, and the angels of God ascending and descending upon the Son of Man."

What gifts did Jesus flow in?

_____ of Knowledge

P_____

Hearing God's Voice For Kids Journal

✓ *Each child will listen to hear what the Lord would say to them personally. You will need to pray with them first and encourage them to ask the Holy Spirit to come and speak the Father's heart for them. Children have less inhibition than adults when it comes to how God feels about them. Encourage them to allow the Father to love on them.*

Writing the thoughts of God

_____

_____

_____

_____

_____

_____

_____

_____

_____

_____

_____

_____

_____

_____

Hearing God's Voice For Kids Journal

Let's think about the nine gifts of the Spirit. Here are some clues. See if you can tell by the picture which gift we are thinking about.

W_____
___
W_____

W_____
___
K_____

F_____

Hearing God's Voice For Kids Journal

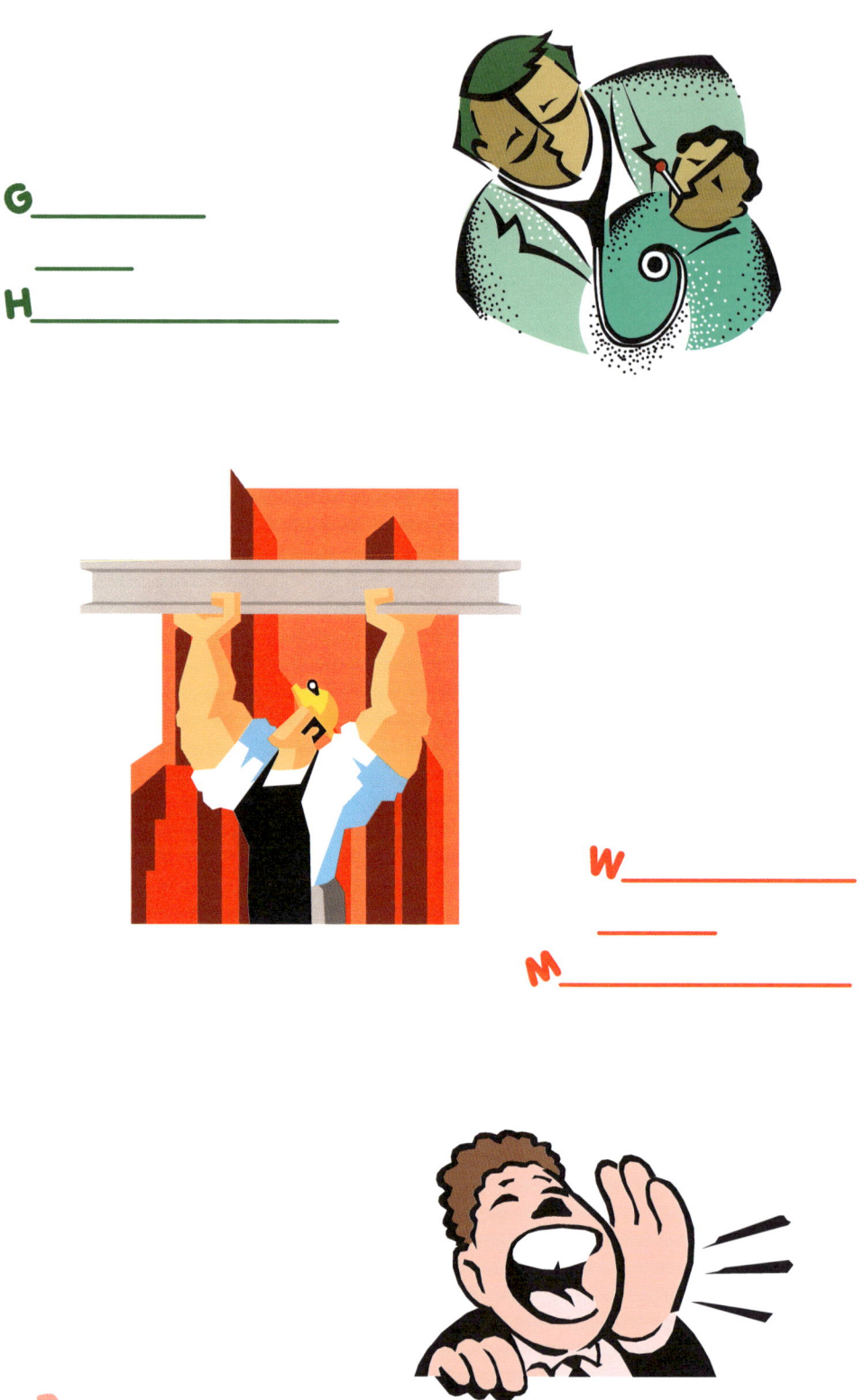

G_____
___
H_____

W_____
___
M_____

P_____

Hearing God's Voice For Kids Journal

D_____
   _____
S_____

D_____
K_____
   _____
T_____

I_____
   _____
T_____

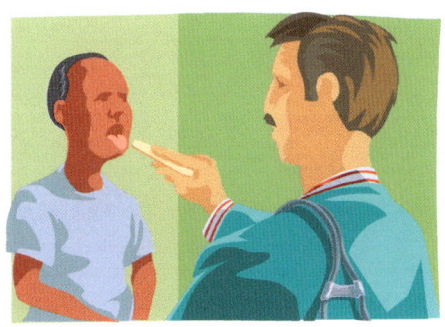

Hearing God's Voice For Kids Journal

Do you remember?

1 Corinthians 14:31
For _____ can _____ prophesy one by one, that _____ may learn and _____ may be encouraged.

Ephesians 5:1
Therefore be imitators of _____ as dear _____.

1 Peter 4:10
As _____ one has received a _____, minister it to one another, as good stewards of the manifold grace of God.

Who can prophesy?

Answer- _____

Who has received a gift?

Answer- _____ _____

Who are we to be like?

Answer- _____

Hearing God's Voice For Kids Journal

1 Corinthians 14:1

P_____ LOVE

And

D_____

Spiritual gifts

But

Especially

That you may

P_____

Hearing God's Voice For Kids Journal

Ephesians 5:1

Therefore be

I_____

Of

God

As

Dear

C_____

Hearing God's Voice For Kids Journal

1 Peter 4:10

As each o_____

has received a g_____,

M_____ it (helping)

to one another

As good s_____

of the manifold grace of God.

Hearing God's Voice For Kids Journal

- ✓ Have the children draw a picture of how they feel while learning to hear the voice of God.

Drawing For God

REVIEW

1 Corinthians 14:1

Pursue love, and desire spiritual gifts, but especially that you may prophesy.

1 Corinthians 14:31

For you can all prophesy one by one, that all may learn and all may be encouraged.

Ephesians 5:1

Therefore be imitators of God as dear children.

1 Peter 4:10

As each one has received a gift, minister it to one another, as good stewards of the manifold grace of God.

REVIEW

How do we get to know the voice of God?

#1- We talk to the Holy Spirit and we tell Him we love Him which is what we call worship and relationship.

#2- We ask Him to come which is what we call making room for Him.

#3- Then we wait -which is:

Look to see

Listen to hear

And

Sense to feel

Why do we do this?

*We want to be like Jesus

Other examples the Scriptures give us for Jesus being used in the gifts of the Spirit:

(the * at the end of each portion of Scripture tells which gift Jesus was flowing in)

John 2:1-11

On the third day there was a wedding in Cana of Galilee, and the mother of Jesus was there. Now both Jesus and His disciples were invited to the wedding. And when they ran out of wine, the mother of Jesus said to Him, "They have no wine." Jesus said to her, "Woman, what does your concern have to do with Me? My hour has not yet come." His mother said to the servants, "Whatever He says to you, do it." Now there were set there six waterpots of stone, according to the manner of purification of the Jews, containing twenty or thirty gallons apiece. Jesus said to them, "Fill the waterpots with water." And they filled them up to the brim. And He said to them, "Draw some out now, and take it to the master of the feast." And they took it. When the master of the feast had tasted the water that was made wine, and did not know where it came from (but the servants who had drawn the water knew), the master of the feast called the bridegroom. And he said to him, "Every man at the beginning sets out the good wine, and when the guests have well drunk, then the inferior. You have kept the good wine until now!"

*Faith
*Working of Miracles

John 4:7-19

A woman of Samaria came to draw water. Jesus said to her, "Give Me a drink." For His disciples had gone away into the city to buy food. Then the woman of Samaria said to Him, "How is it that You, being a Jew, ask a drink from me, a Samaritan woman?" For Jews have no dealings with Samaritans. Jesus answered and said to her, "If you knew the gift of God, and who it is who says to you, 'Give Me a drink,' you would have asked Him, and He would have given you living water." The woman said to Him, "Sir, You have nothing to draw with, and the well is deep. Where then do You get that living water? Are You greater than our father Jacob, who gave us the well, and drank from it himself, as well as his sons and his livestock?" Jesus answered and said to her, "Whoever drinks of this water will thirst again, but whoever drinks of the water that I shall give him will never thirst. But the water that I shall give him will become in him a fountain of water springing up into everlasting life." The woman said to Him, "Sir, give me this water, that I may not thirst, nor come here to draw." Jesus said to her, "Go, call your husband, and come here." The woman answered and said, "I have no husband." Jesus said to her, "You have well said, 'I have no husband,' "for you have had five husbands, and the one whom you now have is not your husband; in that you spoke truly." The woman said to Him, "Sir, I perceive that You are a prophet.

*Word of Knowledge

Matthew 9:27-30
When Jesus departed from there, two blind men followed Him, crying out and saying, "Son of David, have mercy on us!" And when He had come into the house, the blind men came to Him. And Jesus said to them, "Do you believe that I am able to do this?" They said to Him, "Yes, Lord." Then He touched their eyes, saying, "According to your faith let it be to you." And their eyes were opened. And Jesus sternly warned them, saying, "See that no one knows it."

*Working of Miracles

Matthew 12:24-25

Now when the Pharisees heard it they said, "This fellow does not cast out demons except by Beelzebub, the ruler of the demons." But Jesus knew their thoughts, and said to them: *"Every kingdom divided against itself is brought to desolation, and every city or house divided against itself will not stand.*

*Discerning of spirits
*Word of Knowledge

Hearing God's Voice For Kids Journal

There are numerous activations to be done to help encourage your children to hear the voice of the Lord. Below are a few listed for you to complete with your children. These can be done more than one time in a sitting to encourage the listening ear, the seeing eye and sensing to feel to be expressed.

- Words of Knowledge – knowledge given by the Lord that you do not already know.
  One example- someone has a headache that the Lord desires to heal.

- Ministering the heart of God to an individual. Divide children into groups of four.
  Example- one person sits in a chair while a team of 3 prays and tells the individual what they sense the Lord is saying to encourage them.

- Pop corn encouragement. Children take turns standing and encouraging someone in the room with what the Lord is saying to them.
  This activation should be quick short words of encouragement that will allow for a number of children to share.

- Class setting- have parents come in at the end of class and let the children minister the heart of the Father to the parents.
  This works best when the children do not know who they are ministering to.

Note to parents and children's workers-
The best way to see your child/children move forward and make progress in hearing the voice of the Lord is to provide a platform for them to exercise this gift. Remember that we can help them in almost any situation to seek to encourage people. While standing in line at a grocery store you can ask your child to encourage the cashier. There is no need to wait until there is a monthly meeting (like we have) to allow your children to use their gift. You, yourself can also seek to encourage people around you. I once told a cashier that God had placed a gift in him to help people and that people would look to him to give wise counsel – and that he would have groups of boys watching him and needing to hear truth. This cashier had just changed his major in college to social work and psychology because he wants to help young boys who need guidance in their life. He was looking for confirmation of the change he had just made. He was so excited about what I said that he asked me to look for him whenever I returned to that store. He also said that it made his day- the best thing he had heard in a long time and that he would not forget how good it made him feel. I did share with him about the love of God for him. He has a grandmother who is praying for him so it was a good reminder to him.
A great resource to help you train children to hear the voice of God is the adult manual, Getting to Know the Voice of God. I highly recommend it.

Hearing God's Voice For Kids Journal

ANSWER KEY

Page 5- pursue, desire, prophesy

Page 6- imitators, children

Page 7- one, gift, minister, stewards

Page 8- Word, Word, Faith, Gifts, Working, Prophecy, Discerning, Different, Interpretation

Page 12- Jesus

Page 14- Word, Word, Faith, Gifts, Working, Prophecy, Discerning, Different, Interpretation

Page 15- see, hear, feel

Page 16- look, listen, sense

Page 19- Jesus

Page 20- you, all, all, all, all, encourage

Page 21- love, gifts, prophecy

Page 28- wisdom, knowledge, faith, healings, miracles, prophecy, spirits, tongues, tongues

Page 31- Word of Wisdom, Word of Knowledge, Faith

Page 32- Gifts of Healings, Working of Miracles, Prophecy

Page 33- Discerning of Spirits, Different Kinds of Tongues, Interpretation of Tongues

Page 34- you, all, all, all, God, children, each, gift, all, each one, Jesus

Page 35- pursue, desire, prophesy

Page 36- imitators, children

Page 37- one, gift, minister, stewards

Hearing God's Voice For Kids Journal

Made in the USA
Charleston, SC
08 April 2014